KNOW ABOUT
THE TEMPLES OF INDIA

MAPLE KIDS

Know about The Temples of India

Published by

MAPLE PRESS PRIVATE LIMITED
office: A-63, Sector 58, Noida 201301, U.P., India
phone: +91 120 455 3581, 455 3583
email: info@maplepress.co.in
website: www.maplepress.co.in

Reprinted in 2019

ISBN: 978-93-50335-62-8

Contents

Preface

Indian Temples are synthesis of wonderful art & elaborate sculptures, depicting Hindu mythological, enshrined deities to worship, represent the values of Hinduism and a place where man can connect with God spiritually. Indian temples comprises of huge pillared Mandapas with elaborate sculptures, sabas for dancing and wide circumambulating passages with other deities placed around the main deity. This constituted a temple complex.

Worship at the temple is not congregational. Instead, individuals or small groups of devotees approach the sanctum in order to obtain a vision (darshana) of the God, say prayers and perform devotional worship. Because the God exists in totality in the shrine, any object that touch the image or even enters the sanctum is filled with power and, when returned to their givers, it confers the grace of the divine on the human world. Only-persons of requisite purity who have been specially trained are able to handle the power of the deity. Hence, the temple sanctums are operated by priests who take the offerings from worshippers, present them directly to the image of the deity and then return most of the gifts to the devotees for use or consumption later at home.

This book jots down the most famous temples and pilgrimages of India along with brief information on each.

CHAPTER 1
Khajuraho

Location of the site: Khajuraho, Madhya Pradesh

Famous for. Khajuraho is well known for erotic art sculptures, carved temples and Dance Festival

Significance: World Heritage Site

Nearby attractions: Panna Wildlife Sanctuary

Even if situated in the middle of nowhere, the Khajuraho temple complex site is one of the most popular places of both foreign and Indian tourists. Temples of Khajuraho hold the attention of a visitor with their sculptural art, which is so exquisite and intricate, that one cannot even dream of cloning it now. Perfect in execution and sublime in expressions, these Khajuraho temples are a dedicated to the womanhood. The artist's creative instincts have beautifully captured various facets and moods of life on stone.

Khajuraho, the ancient 'Kharjjuravahaka', was the principal seat of authority of the Chandella rulers who adorned it with numerous tanks, scores of lofty temples of sculptural grace and architectural splendor. The local tradition lists eighty-five temples but now only twenty-five are standing examples in various stages of preservation. But for Chausath-Yogini, Brahma and Mahadeva, which are of granite, all the other temples are of fine-grained sandstone, buff, pink or Dale yellow in colour.

Khajuraho Temples - A Celebration of Life The existing temple of Khajuraho can be divided into three groups, Western, Eastern and Southern. The famous Western Group, designated a World Heritage site, is enclosed within a beautifully laid-out park. Yasovarman (AD 954) built the temple of Lord Vishnu, now famous as Lakshmana temple is an ornate and an evolved example of its time proclaiming the prestige of the Chandellas.

The Vishvanatha, Parsvanatha and Vaidyanatha temples in Khajuraho belong to the time of king Dhanga, the successor of Yasovarman. The Jagadambi, Chitragupta, are noteworthy among the western group of royal temples of Khajuraho.

The largest and grandest temple of Khajuraho is the immortal Kandariya Mahadeva, which is attributed to king Ganda (AD 1017-29).

The other examples that followed viz., Vamana, Adinatha, Javari, Chaturbhuj and Duladeo, are smaller but elaborately designed. The Khajuraho groups of temples are noted for lofty terraces (jagati) and functionally effective plans. The sculptural embellishments include, besides the cult images, 'Parivara', 'Parsva', 'Avarana', 'Devatas', 'Dikpalas', the 'Apsaras' and 'Sura-Sundaris' which win universal admiration for their delicate, youthful female forms of ravishing beauty. The attire and ornamentation embrace the winsome grace and charm.

CHAPTER 2
Birla Mandir, Delhi

Location: Delhi
Built by: Baldeo Das Birla
Devoted to: Laxmi and Narayan

The Laxmi Narayan Mandir (temple) built by B.D. Birla is a modern Hindu temple dedicated to Laxmi (goddess of wealth) and Narayana (the preserver). It was inaugurated by Mahatma Gandhi with the stipulation that it should be open to all castes (including the untouchables) and all faiths, so it is more welcoming to foreigners than the average temple.

History

This temple was built over a six year period (1933 - 1939) and was opened by Mahatma Gandhi.

Temple, architecture

The highest tower in the temple reaches a height of 165 feet while the ancillary towers reach 116 feet. The Geeta Bhavan, a hall, is adorned with beautiful paintings depicting scenes from Indian mythology. There is also a temple dedicated to Buddha in this complex with fresco paintings describing his life and work. The entire complex, especially the walls and the upper gallery are full of paintings carried out by artists from Jaipur in Rajasthan. The rear of the temple has been developed as an artificial mountainous landscape with fountains and waterfalls.

Significance

This is one of the landmarks in the nation's capital New Delhi. It was built in the 20th century by the Birla family, the family of industrialists known for its many other temples in India. It is modern in concept and construction. It attracts several devotees and international tourists. The presiding deity here is Lakshmi Narayan (Vishnu).

Other Shrines in the temple

Durga and Shiva are the other major deities housed in this temple.

CHAPTER 3
Konark Sun Temple

Location: Konark, Orissa
Also known as: Black Pagoda and Konark
Built by: King Narsingha Deva
Presiding Deity: Surya or The Sun God

Kainapara of the 1st century AD, is an important port of the Orissa coast. The most notable marvel of Orissan art is the stately Sun Temple of Konark. Built in AD 1250, during the reign of the Eastern Ganga King Narasimhadeva

-I (AD 1238-64), it was to enshrine an image of Sun ('Arka'), the patron deity of the place.

The Chariot Temple - Temple of The Sun

The entire temple complex in Konark was designed in the form of a huge chariot drawn by seven spirited horses on twelve pairs of exquisitely carved wheels. The sanctum symbolizes the majestic stride of the Sun God and marks the culmination of the Orissan architectural style.

There are two rows of 12 wheels on each side of the Konark sun temple. Some say the wheels represent the 24 hours in a day and others say the 12 months. The seven horses are said to symbolize the seven days of the week. There is a dancing hall here, an audience hall and a high tower too. Europeon Sailors called this Sun Temple of Konarak, the Black Pagoda due to its dark colour and magnetic power that drew ships into the shore and caused shipwrecks.

The Vimana of the Duel has collapsed, while those of Jagamohana and the Nata-Mandapa are better preserved. The walls of the Sun temple in

Konark contain superb carving of divine, semi-divine, human and animal figures amidst floral and geometric ornamentations.

The vivacious Kanyas and danseuse are remarkable for their sensuous modeling, pulsating with human emotions which are absorbed in a variety of gestures and rhythmic actions. Such sculptures render the Orissan temple a class into themselves. Mighty Simha-Gajas welcome the visitor at the porches. The Sun Temple belongs to the medieval period, embellished with intricate carvings both on the inside and outside. Visit this interesting Konark sun temple dedicated to the Sun God, located in the town of Konark, in the Orissa.

CHAPTER 4
Meenakshi Temple

Madurai or 'the city of nectar' is the oldest and second largest city of Tamil Nadu. This city is located on Vaigai River Bank and was the capital of Pandyan rulers. The Pandyan king, Kulasekhara had built a gorgeous temple around which he created a lotus shaped city. It has been a centre of learning and pilgrimage, for centuries. Legend has it, that the divine nectar falling from Lord Shiva's locks, gave the city its name - 'Madhurapuri', now known as 'Madurai'.

The Sri Meenakshi Sundareswara temple and Madurai city originated together. According to tradition, Indra once committed sin when he killed a demon, who was then performing penance. He could find no relief from remorse in his own kingdom. He came down to earth. While passing through a forest of Kadamba trees in Pandya land, he felt relieved of his burden. His servitors told him that there was Shivalinga under a Kadamba tree beside the lake. Certain, that it was the Linga that had helped him, he worshipped it and built a small temple around it. It is believed that it is this Linga, which is still under worship in the Madurai temple. The shrine is called the 'Indra Vimana'.

Once Dhananjaya, a merchant of Manavur, the place where the Pandyas had arrived after the second deluge in Kumari Kandam, having been overtaken by nightfall in Kadamba forest, spent the night in the Indra Vimana. When next morning he woke up, he was surprised to see signs of worship. Thinking that it must be the work of the Devas, he narrated the incident to the Pandyan King Kulasekhara, in Manavur. Meanwhile, Lord Shiva had instructed Pandya in a dream to build a temple and a city at the spot Dhananjaya would indicate. Kulasekhara, when heard from Dhananjaya, executed the instructions of Lord Shiva. That's how, originated Sri Meenakshi Sundareswara temple and Madurai city.

When the next Pandya, Malayadhvaja and his queen, Kanchanamala, performed a sacrifice for a child, Lord Shiva caused Goddess Parvati Herself to step out of the fire as a little girl. She had three breasts. Lord Shiva told the couple that the third breast would disappear when she set eyes on he who was to be her husband. They were to name her 'Thadathagai' and bring her up as if she were a boy.

She succeeded her father to the throne at his death. She gained many military victories. Finally she marched on to Kailasa itself. When she saw Lord Shiva, her third breast disappeared. The Lord told her to return to

Madurai and said that He would marry her there. The divine marriage was celebrated. This is the theme much beloved of Madurai artists. There is a superb sculpture of this in the temple. The crowning of Meenakshi, for she was the same as Thadathagai, is celebrated as a festival in the temple.

CHAPTER 5
Chintpurni Temple

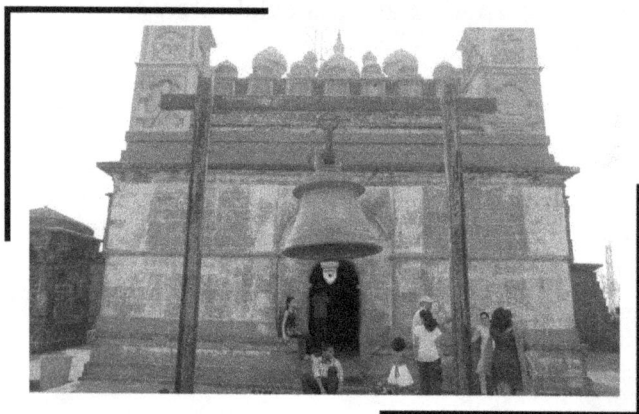

A popular place of pilgrimage, Chintpurni is about 75-km from the town Una and 100-km from Jalandhar.

The Legend Of Chintpurni Temple

Alongwith hundreds of mythical legends about the origin of the temples in different parts of India, the very popular temple of Chintpurni is of the same type. The legend is that one 'Bhagat Mai Dass' was a great devotee of Durga deity worshipped her with great devotion and never bothered over mundane affairs. He was a married man and his family along with others had shifted from Patiala side to village 'Rapoh' in Una district of Himachal Pradesh.

The legend is that one-day Bhagat Mai Dass while going to his father-in-law's place felt tired while passing by a jungle and slept under a tree. He had a dream: a young girl appeared before him and wanted him to stay there and worship her. He woke up in bewilderment.

He returned to the particular spot from his father-in-law's place and went on praying to Durga. The girl appeared this time in human form and told him the whereabouts where he would find her in the form of a 'pindi' (a round stone-ball). He should install the Pindi in a temple. The Devi blessed him that he would have no fright, as it was a 'Devasthan', (site of Gods) though so deserted. She disappeared and Bhagat Mai Das discovered the Pindi and installed it in a temple.

It is believed that the place is where the toes of 'Sati' Goddess fell after being cut off by the 'Chakra' of Lord Vishnu, when he was cutting away the pieces of Sati's dead body carried by Lord Shiva in his Tandava Nritya'. The Pindi represents Sati's feet and is a manifestation of her. Chintpurni Devi is believed to fulfill the desires of a person who comes there and devotedly worships her.

The temple is very popular and attracts thousands of pilgrims every year. The jungle has almost disappeared. The Mantram repeated in the 'Puja' is said to have been revealed by the Devi herself when she appeared in human form.

The main fair is held during the 10 days of 'Shukla paksh' in August, in addition to many other religious festivals. In recent years the temple has been renovated with the help of major donations from devotees all over the country.

CHAPTER 6
Brihadeesvarar Temple

The most enduring aspect of the four-century rule of the Cholas was the extensive temple building they undertook, creating a sacred circuit of 108 Shiva temples in the Kaveri Delta. The most celebrated Shiva temple of all, appropriately called Brihadeesvara and Daksinameru, is the grandest creation of the Chola emperor Rajaraja (AD 985-1012). It was inaugurated by the king himself in his 19th regal year (AD 1009-10) and named it after himself as 'Rajeswara Peruvudaiyar'.

Architecturally, it is the most ambitious structural temple built of granite. Brihadeesvara Temple is within a spacious inner Prakara of 240.90m long (east-west) and 122m broad (north-south), with a Gopura at the east and three other ordinary 'Torana' entrances one at each lateral sides and the third at rear. The Prakara is surrounded by a double-storeyed 'Malika' with 'Parivaralayas'.

The Sikhara, a cupolic dome, is octagonal and rests on a single block of granite, a square of 7.8m weighing 80tons. The majestic 'Upapitha' and 'Adhishthana' are common to all the axially placed entities like the 'Ardhamaha' and 'Mukha-Mandapas' and linked to the main sanctum but approached through a north-south transept across the 'Ardha-Mandapa', which is marked by lofty 'Sopanas'.

The moulded plinth is extensively engraved with inscriptions by its royal builder who refers to his many endowments, pious acts and organizational events connected to Brihadeesvara Temple. The Brihad-Linga within the sanctum is 8.7m high. Life-size iconographic representations on the wall niches and inner passage include Durga, Lakshmi, Saraswati and Bhikshatana, Virabhadra Kalantaka, Natesa, Ardhanarishvara and Alingana forms of Shiva. The mural paintings on the walls of the lower ambulatory inside are finest examples of Chola and later periods.

Sarfoji, a local Maratha ruler, rebuilt the Ganapati shrine. The celebrated Thanjavur School of paintings of the Nayakas are largely superimposed over the Chola murals.

CHAPTER 7
Mahabalipuram
(Mamallapuram)

Mahabalipuram or Mamallapuram, the city of Mamalla, is after the title of great Pallava ruler Narasimhavarman-I (AD 630-68). It was a seaport during the time of 1st century AD and AD 140, many Indian colonists sailed to South-East Asia through this port town.

While there is some evidence of architectural activity going back to the period of Mahendravarman-I (AD 600-30), the father of Mamalla, most of the monuments like rock-cut Rathas, sculptured scenes on open rocks like Arjuna's penance, the caves of Govardhanadhari and Mahishasuramardini, the Jala-Sayana Perumal temple are attributed to the period of Narasimhavarman-I Mamalla.

The monolithic Rathas, from single to triple-storeyed, display a variety of architectural forms. The Dharmaraja, Arjuna and Draupadi Rathas are square on plan, the Bhima and Ganesha Rathas are rectangular while Sahadeva Ratha apsidal. Though monolithic sculpturing, both cut-in and cut-out, continued even during later periods, the structural architecture was introduced on a grand scale by Pallava Rajasimha (AD 700-28), culminating in erection of the world famous Shore temple in Mahabalipuram.

After Rajasimha, there is a lull in the architectural activity of the place, except a few additions during late-Pallava and Chola times. The grandiose Vijayanagara phase here is represented by the Raja Gopurams and the Sthala-Sayana temple, juxtaposed to the carved boulder of Arjuna's penance.

CHAPTER 8
Jain Temples in India

The temple sites and cave architectures made by the Jains are known for the intricacy and the decor. Jainism as a religious creed had a great hold on Orissa and there is no wonder that there should be a considerable impact of Jainism on the adjoining Purulia district. But, the all in all rock-cut architectural marvels are the caves of Udaygiri and Kandhagiri.

Ranakpur is another amazing example of Jain

monumental splendour. This temple complex is the largest Jain temple in India, covering an area of nearly 4,500 square yards. It lies on the curve of a boulder-strewn river deep in the forested Aravalli hills. Also these temples are known as one of the most beautiful Jain temples, built during the 15th century. Delwara Temples, the celebrated and world famous Jain temples situated in Rajasthan, are carved in marble, the design and accuracy of workmanship is unbelievable.

CHAPTER 9
Lotus Temple, Delhi

"The purpose of places of worship and edifices for adoration is simply that of unity, in order that various nations, divergent races, varying souls, may gather there and among them amity, love and accord may lie realized."

–Baha'i Holy Writings

The Baha'i House of Worship (Lotus Temple) in New Delhi, India, is a symbol manifesting the Baha'i Faith, revealing the simplicity, clarity and freshness of this new religion.

According to the architects of the Lotus Temple, a design was chosen that would be familiar to the Indian people, without imitating any of the architectural styles of India. Hence, the Temple came to be constructed in the shape of the beautiful lotus flower, the national flower of India.

The lotus has always enjoyed an unparalleled popularity throughout the length and breadth of India from the earliest times down to the present day, as shown by its pre-dominance in literature and art. Mentioned in the oldest Veda, it plays a prominent part in the mythology of Brahmanism. To the later Sanskrit poets, it is the emblem of beauty to which they constantly compare the faces of their heroines. The lotus, moreover, enters into Indian art of all ages and all religions as a prominent decorative element. It appears on the oldest architectural monuments of Hinduism all over India. With the spread of Buddhism to the countries of the Far East, its use as an ornament in religious art has extended as far as Japan.

Breathtaking architecture

Around the lotus-shaped dome, which houses the assembly area, are walkways with curved balustrades, bridges and stairs, which surround the nine pools representing the floating leaves of the lotus. Apart from serving an obvious aesthetic function, the pools also help ventilate the building.

The lotus, as seen from outside, has three sets of leaves or petals, all of which are made out of thin concrete shells. The outermost set of nine petals, called the 'entrance leaves', open outwards and form the nine entrances all around the outer hall. The next set of nine petals, called the 'outer leaves', point inwards.

The entrance and outer leaves together cover the outer hall. The third set of nine petals, called the 'inner leaves', appear to be partly closed. Only the tips open out, somewhat like a partly opened bud. This portion, which rises above the rest, forms the main structure housing the central hall. Since the lotus is open at the top, a glass-and-steel roof provides protection from rain and facilitates the entry of natural light into the auditorium.

CHAPTER 10
Kali Temple, Dakshineswar

The Dakshineswar temple has an enormous courtyard surrounded by 12 smaller temples dedicated to Lord Shiva.

One of the most visited places of worship in India and a huge tourist attraction of West Bengal, the spectacular Kali temple at Dakshineswar has a most interesting history.

In the year 1847, Rani Rasmani, a wealthy and pious widow, prepared to go upon a long pilgrimage to the sacred city of Banaras (now Varanasi), to express her devotion to the Divine Mother. There being no railway line between Calcutta and Banaras in those days, rich persons made the journey by boat rather than by road. It is said that the convoy of Rani Rasmani consisted of twenty-four boats carrying relatives, servants and supplies.

A Strange Dream

However, the journey that had been prepared for and looked forward to for so long was never taken. The night before the pilgrimage began goddess Kali appeared to the Rani in a dream and said, "There is no need to go to Banaras. Install my statue in a beautiful temple on the banks of the Ganges river and arrange for my worship there. Then I shall manifest myself in the image and accept worship at that place."

Profoundly affected by the dream, the Rani immediately looked for and purchased land and promptly ordered the construction of the temple.

The large temple complex was completed and consecrated in 1855 and the elderly Ramkumar was chosen as the head priest. Within the year this priest died and his responsibility passed to his younger brother, Ramakrishna (later got famous as Sri Ramakrishna Paramahamsa, the great God-Man), who over the next thirty years would bring great fame to the Dakshineswar temple.

Ramakrishna

However, Ramakrishna did not serve for long as the temple's head priest. From the first days of his service in the shrine of the goddess Kali, he was filled with a rare form of the love of God known in Hinduism as maha-bhava. Worshipping in front of the statue of Kali, Ramakrishna would be overcome with such ecstatic love for the deity that he would fall to the ground and, immersed in a spiritual trance, lose all consciousness of the external world. These experiences of God-intoxication became so frequent that he was relieved of his duties as temple priest but allowed to continue living within the temple compound.

During the next twelve years Ramakrishna delved ever deeper into this passionate and absolute love of the divine. His practice was to express such intense devotion to a particular deity that they would physically manifest themselves before him. Shiva, Kali, Radha-Krishna, Sita-Rama, Christ and Mohammed frequently appeared to him and his fame as an avatar or divine incarnation, rapidly spread throughout Bengal.

Ramakrishna died in 1886 at the age of fifty, but his life, his intense spiritual practices and the temple of Kali at Dakshineswar, which was the scene of many of his ecstatic trances, continued to attract pilgrims from all over India and the world. Even today, more than 100 years after these wondrous occurrences, visitors at the temple experience the pure spirit of Ramakrishna Paramahamsa, a perfect blend of the human and the divine.

CHAPTER 11
Tirupati Temple

Location: Tirupati is a town in the Chittoor district of the Southern portion of Andhra Pradesh and is at a convenient train journey away from Chennai (formerly Madras) in Tamil Nadu. Tirumalai, on the last of the seven Hills, is home to this temple and is connected by a well-maintained and picturesque mountain road constructed by the Tirumala Tirupati Devasthanam.

Significance: Tirupati/Tirumala is a pilgrimage centre of great significance and is visited by hundreds and thousands of pilgrims throughout the year. Venkateswara or Srinivasa or Balaji as the presiding deity Vishnu is known, is enshrined in this temple, located on a range of the Eastern Ghats, called the Seven Hills. It is an ancient temple and its glory has been sung by the saints of the yesteryears.

Said to be the richest temple in India, this temple is a vibrant cultural and philanthropic institution with a grand history spanning several centuries. It attracts pilgrims from all over the country and it is not unusual for pilgrims to stand in line for hours together to obtain a glimpse of the presiding deity for a few fleeting seconds.

TTD or Tirumala Tirupati Devasthanam manages the affairs of the temple, the well-being of the pilgrims, the upkeep of the environs in and around the Tirumala hills and sponsors several undertakings that are religious, charitable, social and educational in nature.

References to Tiruvenkatam abound in early Tamil literature (Tolkappiam and Silappadikaram). Explicit reference to the Lord of Tiruvenkatam is found in the works of the early Tamil Saint Poets Poigai Alwar, Bhuthathu Alwar and Pay Alwar as well as in the poems of the later Alwars. The great religious leader Ramanuja Acharya is said to have visited here in the 11th -12th century AD.

References to Venkatachalam are also found in several of the Puranas. Tirumalai constitutes one of the 108 Sri Vaishnava Divya Desams - sacred shrines in the Sri Vaishnavite tradition. Krishna Deva Raya of the Vijayanagar Empire is said to have visited this temple seven times. A statue of Raja Krishnadevaraya is also found in the temple. The Venkatesa Itihasa Mala and the Varaha Purana contain several legends connected with Tirumalai.

The Temple

The temple of Lord Venkateswara is built on top of Seshachala hill, one of the seven hills known as the Thirumalai hills. The temple covers an area of about two acres. The sanctum is 12 feet square housing the image of the Lord. It is topped with a golden vimanam called the Ananda Nilaya Vimanam. This three-tiered tower is about 38 feet high. The entrance Gopuram is about 50 feet high and faces east.

The deity is worshipped as Sri Venkateswar or Venkatachalapathy and the image is in standing posture on a pedestal of lotus flower. The image is adorned with ornaments studded with precious stones and gems. There are also images of Krishna, Rama, Sita and Lakshmana in the sanctum. Sri Devi and Boodevi both adorn the Lord's chest in the form of two images sculptured in gold.

CHAPTER 12
Sri Rangam

Sri Rangam, the largest Vaishnavite temple in Tamil Nadu, is dedicated to Sri Ranganatha Perumal. This temple is as holy and venerable to Vaishnavites as Chidambaram temple is to Saivites.

Location: Sri Rangam town itself has a railway station on the Madras-Tiruchirapalli line. It is about 5 km from Tiruchirapalli and about 315 km from Chennai. Tiruchirapalli being a large city is well served by road, rail and air. Pilgrims throng to this temple throughout the year, but the main festival falls in December/January during 'Vaikuntha ekathasi' and is conducted over a period of 20 days.

Legends

There are so many legends associated with this temple. One of them relates how the 'Ranga Vimanam' believed to be the chariot of Lord Vishnu came to be installed here. Ikshavahu the descendant of Surya, the Sun god and forebear of Rama, performed a penance in order to obtain the Ranga Vimanam to install it in a temple in Ayodya. Garuda, the mount of Lord Vishnu, delivered the Ranga Vimanam to Ikshavahu. The people of Ayodya thus, venerated and worshipped this Ranga Vimanam for centuries until Lord Vishnu himself was born as Rama in Ayodya as heir to the Surya dynasty.

Rama is the hero of Ramayana, the epic story in which he was banished from his kingdom for 14 years. During this time his wife Sita was abducted by Ravana, the King of Lanka. Vibhishana, the brother of Ravana, helped Rama to defeat and kill Ravana and rescue Rama's wife Sita. At the end of his 14 years of banishment, Rama returned to Ayodya to reclaim his rightful crown. Many kings and others were invited to the coronation and Vibhishana was an important guest. At the end of the ceremony as custom dictated gifts were exchanged. Vibhishana to whom Rama owed a debt of gratitude, presented him with the Ranga Vimanam to be taken to his kingdom, Lanka. On his way Vibhishana arrived near Kaveri River in the South and wanted to perform his daily pooja. He gave the Ranga Vimanam to a boy standing nearby with instructions not to put it on the ground. He got into the river for his ablution and when he came out he found that the boy had put the Ranga Vimanam on the ground. He tried to lift it but failed to move it. He became distraught and prayed to Lord Vishnu who appeared and told him that He wished that the Ranga Vimanam stayed at that spot. The King and others on learning this requested Vibhishana to install the Ranga Vimanam on that spot and perform the 'Adhi Brahmotsava', thereby, consecrating that place. The King who was a great devotee of Lord Vishnu, was delighted with this and built a large temple to house the Ranga Vimanam and called the deity Lord Sri Ranganathar.

CHAPTER 13
Madurai

The name 'Madurai' evokes in the minds of the Tamils the golden era when their language, culture and arts flourished under the patronage of successive Pandian kings. The city was the home of such illustrious institutions as the 'Sangam' which revived and nurtured great works of Tamil poets and artists. It now houses the largest temple complex in Tamil Nadu built by the Nayaka Kings who ruled Madurai from the 16th to 18th century. They have left an indelible imprint of their glorious period in the Meenakshi-Sundareswarar temple. The goddess Sakthi rules the world as Meenakshi in Madurai, as Kamakshi in Kanchi and as Visalakshi in Kasi. But the most revered and worshipped of these three is the Goddess Meenakshi of Madurai.

Location: Madurai has a small airport served by flights from Chennai, Thiruvananthapuram and Mumbai. It is about 16 Km south of the city. There are four bus stands serving local towns and towns afar. The inter-state buses arrive at the TTC bus-stand, which is nearest to the centre of the town. The railway station is just west of the temple complex.

The Temple

At first glance the most striking feature of the temple is the soaring 'gopuram' (gateway towers) built above the four entrances on the four sides. The most popular entrance is on the East Side through a towerless entrance in line with the shrine of Goddess Meenakshi. This entrance leads to the 'Ashtasakthi Mandapam' where the pillars are full of sculptures, illustrating the different aspects of Goddess Meenakshi and the miracles performed by Lord Siva in Madurai. This hall leads to the 'Ciththirai gopuram' passing through which will take you to a passageway on the eastern end of the 'Pottramarai kulam' (The Golden Lotus Pond). Steps go down on all four sides of this pond to the water in the middle of which stands a brass column. Walking around the pond in a clock-wise direction brings into view the golden 'vimanam' of the shrines of Goddess Meenakshi and Lord Sundareswarar while on the east of the pond. As you come round the tank you pass the 'Oonjal mandapam' where every Friday, Goddess Meenakshi and Lord Sundareswarar arc put on a swing while 'othuvars' sing the ancient Tamil hymns. Passing the 'Oonjal mandapam' you arrive at the 'Kilikkoottu mandapam' where parrots were used to be kept. Next is the entrance to Goddess Meenakshi shrine. North of the entrance to Meenakshi temple is the entrance to Sundareswarar temple.

Opening times and festivals

The temple is open for worship throughout the day. There are festivals in this temple practically every month. Two main festivals fall in the month of Chiththirai (April/May) and in Aavani (August/September).

The temple abounds with sculptures depicting the various lore of Hindu mythology. The dancing pose of Lord Natarajar usually has the left leg raised. In the 'Hall of Silver' (Velliamblam) there is a statue of Lord Natarajar with his right leg raised, which is very unusual. Near the Southern tower there are five musical pillars made up of 22 slender rods.

Each of these rods gives out a different note when tapped gently. The pillar is carved out of a single piece of granite stone.

CHAPTER 14
Amarnath

Situated in a narrow gorge at the farther end of Lidder Valley, Amarnath stands at 3,888 m. and is 46 km from Pahalgam and 141 km from Srinagar. And the distance between Pahalgam and Srinagar is 96 km.

Though the original pilgrimage subscribes that the yatra be undertaken from Srinagar, the more common practice is to begin journey at Chandanwari and cover the distance to

Amarnath and back in five days. Amarnath is considered to be one of the major Hindu Dhams. The holy cave is the abode of the holy trinity, Lord Shiva. The guardian of the absolute, Lord Shiva, the destroyer, is enshrined in the form of an ice-lingam in this cave located at farther end of the Lidder Valley. This lingam is formed naturally of an ice stalagmite, which wakes up and wanes with the moon.

The Yatra

The trek to Amarnath begins at Srinagar on the panchami day of the bright half of the month. The next halt enroute is Pampur, 9 miles south east of Srinagar. Subsequent halts are at Avanripur, Brijbihara and Martand. Martand is known for its ancient temple dedicated to the Sun God - now in ruins. Enroute to Martand are Anant Nag and Gautam Nag. Martand is known as the architectural lion of Kashmir. It is a temple with a colonnade of 84 columns full of artistic work. This temple dates back to the reign of King Lalitaditya of Kashmir of the 8th century. The next halt is at Aishmukam and the next is Pahalgam, which is reached on the day of Dasami, the tenth day of the bright half of the month. At Pahalgam is the confluence of the rivers Seshnag and Liddar. The next stop enroute is Chandanwadi, where, is the confluence of the rivers Asthan Marg and Seshnag. Further up is the Pishu Ghati, believed, to be the site where the demons were crushed by the Gods. Further up is the Seshnag lake at a height: Of about 12000 feet above sea level. The Seshnag river flows out of this lake.

The next halt is at Wavjan before the steep climb to the Mahagunus Pass at a height of 14000 feet, after which there is a down slope leading to Panchatarni. From here, the Amarnath cave is reached on the full moon day and the pilgrimage is complete.

Climate

The climatic conditions are very uncertain. Rain or snowfall may take place at any time or place during the Yatra. It is to be particularly noted that abrupt changes in temperature might occur. Sunny weather may turn into rain or snow fall within a short period of time. The temperature may fall up to -50c.

CHAPTER 15
Vaishno Devi

Nestled in the folds of the mighty Trikuta mountain, 61 kilometres north of Jammu at a height of 5,200 feet from the sea level, the cave shrine of Trikuta Bhagwati has been a beacon of faith and fulfillment for millions of devotees since time immemorial.

Vaishno Devi, a holy cave shrine situated at an altitude of over 5000 feet in a beautiful recess of the Trikuta mountains forming a part of the lower Himalayas attracts a huge number of pilgrims every day of the year unless the route is blocked by snowfall.

Within the cave are ancient images of three deities, the Mahakali, Mahalakshmi and Mahasaraswati. Popular belief holds that anybody who walks up to the shrine of Vaishno Devi to ask for a boon rarely goes back disappointed. There are many who journey here year after year to pay obeisance, regardless of their faith or belief, creed or class, caste or religion, for Mata Vaishno Devi transcends all such barriers.

Yatra

The Yatra (Religious Pilgrimage) begins in Katra at 1,700 ft. From here, pilgrims have to get a mandatory Yatra slip, which is free of cost from the Yatra Registration Counter at the Tourism Reception Centre.

The Yatra traverses a distance of 7 miles, covering a vertical height of about 3500 ft. The path is wide, tiled and well lit at night. Pure vegetarian food and drinking water is available at outlets along the route, public utilities are also available on the route.

At Bhawan, pilgrims need to present the Yatra slip at the Registration Office and obtain a batch number, which determines your place in the queue for darshan (holy vision). Here, pilgrims take bath and proceed further. Luggage and leather items need to be booked in the cloakrooms.

Baan Ganga

Going down for about a mile, one crosses Baan Ganga, a stream associated with Maa Vaishno Devi. Actually from this place the stiff ascent on the Trikuta range starts. The pilgrims take a purificatory dip in this stream before starting on the ascent. This place is about two and a half kilometers distant from Katra at an altitude of 2,800 ft. above the sea level.

Mata's Cave

Mata's cave shrine is nestled in snow-capped mountains and forests of Trikuta mountain forming a part of the lower Himalayas and 61 kilometers north of Jammu at a height of 5,200 feet above the sea level in the state of Jammu and Kashmir. There is a 13km mountain hike on foot from Katra to the holy shrine of Mata Vaishno Devi. On reaching 'bhawan', token of prashad can be bought and 'snan' can be done before entering the cave for 'darshan'.

It is believed that a supernatural power takes over every soul to terrain the distance with ease.

Bhairon Mandir

It is believed that the journey to Mata's shrine is complete only after visiting the shrine of Bhairon, 2.5 km from the Bhawan, on your way back. You have to collect your belongings before going to this shrine, as the return path from the Bhairon shrine joins the main path at Sanji Chatt.

CHAPTER 16
Chamunda Devi

Chamunda Devi is a Shakti shrine, 10 km west of Palampur, on the Baner River. This colourful shrine has a wrathful form of Durga or Chamunda. The idol in the temple is considered so sacred that it is completely hidden beneath a red cloth.

It is situated on the bank of Baan Ganga. With all the natural surroundings ideally suited for meditation, prayers and spiritual attainments. This was the cremation ground for 22 villages and supposed to be a place, which gives solace, spiritual attainments in the form of Mahakali Chamunda.

Here, Lord Shiva is believed to be present in the form of death, destruction and dead bodies along with Devi Chamunda. Devotees offer prayers, worship and give offerings for their ancestors. It is believed to be sacred to take a dip in River Baan Ganga and to read or recite the writings of Shat Chandi. In the old days, people also used to offer sacrifices to the deity. Kanyas (unmarried baby girls) are worshiped. Also Lord Shiva is worshiped with Holy water from Baan Ganga.

The Past

Chamunda Devi is located at a spot where the famous battle described in the Devi Mahatmyam took place. It is heard that Kali killed the two generals of Shumbha and Nishumba. Their names were Chanda and Munda. As a result of this battle Kali received the name Chamunda. The temple was originally located in a dangerous remote spot. Later, it was relocated to its current location.

Around 400 years ago, the king and a Brahmin priest prayed to Devi for permission to move the temple to some easily accessible location. Devi appeared to the priest in a dream giving her consent. She directed him to dig in a certain spot and an ancient idol would be found and that idol should be installed in the temple and worshipped as Her form.

The king sent out men to bring the idol. Although they were able to locate it but were not able to lift it. Again Devi appeared to the priest in a dream. She explained that the men could not lift the holy relics because they considered it an ordinary stone. She instructed him to get up early in the morning, take a bath, wear fresh clothes and go to the place in a respectful manner. He did as he was told and found that he could easily lift what a large group of men could not. He told the people that it was the power of the Goddess that brought the idol to the temple. In the temple, now you can see scenes from the Devi Mahatmya, Ramayana and Mahabharata. On either side of the Devi's image is Hanuman and Bhairo.

CHAPTER 17
Dwarkadhish Temple

Location: Dwarka, Gujarat.
Also known as: Jagat Mandir.
Dedicated to: Lord Krishna.
Major festivity: During Janmashtami in August.
Lord Krishna's abode

Jagat Mandir, with the presiding deity Shri Krishna is also known as Dwarkadheesh. This temple is an imposing edifice and a superb architectural monument. Having a plinth area of 1800 square feet, the temple consists of a shrine that is supported by 60 pillars of granite and sandstone.

The seven-storey edifice gradually rises to a height of 170 feet. The temple's spire is unique for the view it presents and the experience it induces. Beautifully sculpted sandstone wall enthralls the visitors and the ambulating devotees.

On the west side of the temple is the seat of Adi Shankaracharya, the great master of Hindu faith who visited the temple in the seventh century. For the scholars, a wall poster depicting the family tree tracing the lineage to Lord Krishna offers an interesting insight into the great Indian epic of the Mahabharata.

Legend

An interesting legend surrounds the idol installed at this temple. It is said that, taking pity on his old devotee Badana, who used to traverse the long distance from Dakor to Dwarka, God in the form of an idol went with him to Dakor. This enraged the priests at Dwarka, who chased

Badana to retrieve the idol. Badana persuaded the priests to leave the deity in return of gold, where upon the priests agreed to withdraw. By a miracle, the idol became as light as the nose-ring, which was all that the poor widow could offer.

But the Lord did not want to disappoint the priests. He, therefore, granted them a boon that they will find a replica in Dwarka on a particular day. Unable to resist their curiosity, the priests excavated at the suggested site a little too early, and found yet to grow idol, which is now enshrined at Dwarka.

Historical Evidence

The present shrine is not likely to be older than the Mughal period. The inscriptions on the pillars and other places do not appear to be older than the 15th century AD. There must have been an older shrine, which was probably destroyed by Mahmud Begada in \ 473 AD. The present temple was probably constructed during the period of the great Mughal Emperor Akbar.

CHAPTER 18
ISKCON

The International Society for Krishna Consciousness (ISKCON) was initially raised as a spiritual society in New York to propagate the message of the Bhagwad Gita. Bhaktivedanta Swami Prabhupada is the founder Acharya of the Hare Krishna movement. In India there are about 40 ISKCON temples. Contemplating the traditions of the ancient Vaishnava tradition, its philosophy and practice, these spiritual temples have left a mark on all mankind. Visiting these temples proves to be a pleasant and revealing experience.

Iskcon temple dedicated to the Lord Krishna is built on a hilly place by the Hare-Rama Hare-Krishna cult followers. Completed in 1998, this complex Temples Architecture is one of the largest temples, standing at Hari Krishna Hill, Sant Nagar Main Road, East of Kailash, Delhi, India. Currently the main attraction of the temple is the Robert, who enacts and preaches the Gita.

The magnificent temple has 'Shikharas' at a height of 90-feet above the ground level. The hall of the temple is centrally air-conditioned with a capacity to accommodate about 1,500 people. Beautiful would describe the architecture of the temple mildly, at the entrance are two statues of the guards of Vaikunth (the place where Shri Krishna resides). There are beautiful paintings of Russian artists on the different past times of Radha Krishna, Sita, Ram, Laxman, Hanuman and Chaitanya Mahaprabhu. Special programmes like kirtan, aarti, pravachan and prasadam are held every Sunday between noon to 3.00 pm.

Main Attraction

Usually in August, Krishan Janamashtami Special programmes like kirtan, aarti, pravachan and prasadam are held till morning. Generally, the temple remains open in the morning from 4.30 am to 12.00 pm and then in the evening from 4.00 pm to 9.00 pm. Before you leave don't forget to take the prasad, which is a Dona of nutritious khichdi. The temple is one of the most beautiful and well-maintained ones in Delhi.

CHAPTER 19
Badrinath

Situated in the lofty Himalayan heights in the Tehri-Garhwal hill tracks (Uttarakhand) at the height of 10,248 feet above sea level. The route to Badrinath is one of the most arduous one due to the lofty hilly terrain, curves and cliffs amidst the most scenically beautiful place on the earth. Badrinath dhaam is considered as one of the most sacred centres of pilgrimage.

The temple's present structure was built by the Kings of Garhwal about two centuries ago. The temple has three sections - Garbhagriha (Sanctum), The Darshan Mandap and Sabha Mandap. The Garbhagriha (Sanctum) houses Lord Badri Narayan, Kuber (God of wealth), Natad Rishi, Uthavar, Nar & Narayan.

Lord Badri Narayan (also called as Badri Vishal) is armed with Shankh (Conch) and Chakra in two arms in a lifted posture and two arms rested on the lap in Yogatnudra. The principal image is of black stone and it represents Vishnu seated in a meditative pose. The temple also houses Garuda (Vahana - vehicle of Lord Narayan) and Goddess Mahalaxmi. Also here are the idols of Adi Shankar, Swami Desikan and Shri Ramanujan. Guru-Shisya parampara is supposed to have its roots here.

As per the tradition-decided by Lord Brahma, the temple would be open for six months, i.e as per Hindu calendar from the month of Vaishaka to Karthik, for darshan to common people. For the remaining six months, i.e. from Margashsish to Chaitra the temple would be closed for darshan by common people as it is Devas turn for Lord's darshan.

The Legend

When River Ganges was requested to descend to earth to help the suffering humanity, the earth was too feeble to bear the force of this descent. Hence the mighty river was split into twelve channels, one of them being Alaknanda, which later became the abode of Lord Vishnu or Badrinath.

The present temple was built about two centuries ago by the kings of Garhwal. The principal idol in the temple is of black stone and represents Vishnu seated in a meditative pose and flanked by Nara-Narayan. Badrinath is also known as Vishal Badri and is one of the Panch Badris.

CHAPTER 20
Bull Temple

The 'Bull Temple' is found in Bangalore, the capital of Karnataka. The bull or 'Nandi' is honoured as Shiva's mount in this temple, on the same platform as the Vishvanath Temple. It is also called 'Nandi temple'. The temple has a giant statue of Nandi, carved out of a single boulder. It is a sculptural masterpiece. In Kannada, Basava means bull, which gives the name Basavanagudi to the locality. It faces the

Shiva temple. A statue of Nandi, the bull of Shiva is inside flanked at the back with statues of God Surya and Goddess Chandra on their chariots drawn by horses. Non-Hindus are not allowed in the temple. The temple is always busy with some ceremony or the other going on. On weekends there are musicians who are performing at the temple. Due to the huge monolithic statue of the sitting bull, this temple draws a large number of people every day.

Architecture

The Bull temple located at Basavanagudi is built by Kempe Gowda (one of the rulers under the Vijayanagara Empire during 16th Century and founder of Bengaluru), is a typical example of the Dravidian-style temple. The huge monolithic statue of Nandi in this temple is 4.5m tall and 6m long. This magnificent Nandi has been carved out of a single granite rock. This is one of the oldest temples in Bengaluru situated in Basavanagudi dedicated to Nandi, the mount of Lord Shiva.

It is believed that the source of the river Vishwa Bharathi originates from the feet of the Nandi. The bull has a small iron plate on its head to prevent it, as tradition says, from growing. Farmers offer the first groundnuts harvested to the sacred bull.

Also there is a Ganesh temple, with a large deity made of 110 kilos of butter. The deity of butter is broken up and distributed to the devotees every four years .

Bhoganandeeswara temple

The Bhoganandeeswara temple at the foothills of Nandi Hills goes back to the period of the Banas, Cholas, Hoysalas and the Vijayanagar Kings.

Bhoganandeeswara, Umamaheswara and Arunachaleswara are enshrined here. The kalyanamandapa is of great beauty here. The Yoganandeeswara temple atop the hill goes back to the Chola period. It received extensive patronage from the Vijayanagar Kings. The pillars and metalwork deserve special mention.

The image has been carved out of single granite rock. The original colour of Nandi bull was grey which has now turned black due to the application of coconut oil by the devotees. The statue of the bull has been carved out of a single rock.

Main Attraction

In November & December every year, when the groundnuts have been harvested, Kadalekayi Parishe (The Groundnut fair) is held near the temple. The first groundnuts harvested are offered by the farmers to the sacred bull. Dodda Ganapati, a magnificent image of the Lord, is enshrined adjacent to the Nandi temple.

CHAPTER 21
Somnath Temple- Gujarat

The Somnath in the Prabhas Kshetra in Saurashtra, on the western coast of Gujarat, (INDIA) is one of the twelve Jyotirlingas that are most scared to the Hindus. It is as old as creation and its reference is available in Rig Veda also. It is said - the Moon (Soma) with his wife Rohini worshipped the deity of the temple, the Sparsha Ling, to free himself from the curse of his father-in-law, Daksha Prajapati.

Lord Shiva pleased with his penance restored his light for half of the month. Hence, the deity here is known as Someshwar or Somnath, Lord of the moon and the place as Prabhas.

The Somnath is known as the Shrine Eternal as it has withstood the shocks of time and the attacks of the destroyers. It has risen like a phoenix each time it was destroyed or desecrated. The present temple is reconstructed seventh time at the original site. Sardar Vallabhbhai Patel, the great son of India and its first Deputy Prime Minister, took a pledge on November 13, 1947 for its reconstruction which was completed on December 1, 1995 when the President of India, Dr. Shankar Dayal Sharma dedicated it in the service of the nation. The present temple is built by Shree Somnath Trust, which looks after the entire complex of Shree Somnath and its environs.

Kailash Mahameru Prasada

The Present Temple, Kailash Mahameru Prasada, is built in the Chalukya style of temple architecture and reflects the inherent skill of

Sompuras, Gujarat's master masons. It has the Shikhar portion, the Garbh Gruh, the Sabha Mandap and the Nritya Mandap. Such a temple has not been constructed in India during the last 800 years. The Temple is situated at such a place that there is no land in between from Somnath seashore to Antartica, the South Pole. Such an inscription in Sanskrit is found on the arrow-pillar erected on the sea-protection wall at the Somnath Temple. The Prabhas Kshetra is one of the most sacred places in India for Shaivaites as well as for Vaishnavites. Lord Krishna was hurt here at Bhalka in his foot by the arrow of a hunter who mistook him to be a deer. There is Bhalka Teerth temple at this sacred place.

The mortal remains of Krishna were cremated at Dehotsarga, on the banks of river Hiren. Shree Somnath Trust has built Dehotsarg canopy and Gita Mandir at Dehotsarga. The Dehotsarg canopy shelters 'Krishna-Charan'. The Trust has taken up the project to develop this sacred place as 'Shree Krishna Neejdham-Prasthan Teerth'. Ahalyeshwar Mahadev Temple built by Queen Ahalyabai, Gita Mandir, Laxmi Narayan temple, Baldev Gufa, Mahaprabhuji's Bethak, Triveni Sangam, Parshuram Kshetra, Sun Temple, Prachi and Shashibhushan temples are other places of religious significance in and around the Somnath Temple.

CHAPTER 22
Kailash Temple, Maharashtra

At Ellora, 34 cave temples were carved out of the hillside with hand tools. Only 12 of these 34 caves in the centre are the most impressive. The massive Kailash Temple (cave 16) is nearly one and half times taller than the Parthenon and occupies almost twice its area. It is believed that it was constructed by excavating approximately

200,000 tones of rock and is possibly the world's largest monolithic structure. Representing Lord Shiva's Himalayan home, the temple is exquisitely sculpted with scenes from Hindu mythology, each pulsing with drama, energy and passion.

The Kailash Temple is situated near the village of Ellora. It is considered as one of the most astonishing 'buildings' in the history of architecture. This temple is said to be the world's largest monolithic structure carved from one piece of rock. And, equally impressive in their own right is the rock-hewn temples and monasteries of Ellora that lies just 30 kms from Aurangabad. Kailash Temple at cave 16, there is a huge Shiva-Linga (form of Lord Shiva) which is worshiped. It is the biggest building of Ellora Cave Complex.

The Kailasanatha temple literally scooped out of the hillside, has beautiful sculptures from Ramayana and Mahabharatha carved on its walls. Lord Shiva is worshipped in the form of a giant lingam in the garba griha of this temple.

Architecture

It is believed that work on the Kailasha temple began in the mid-8th century and under the direction of King Krishna I (757-775) of the Rashtrakuta dynasty, the rulers of the western Deccan area. One of the India's greatest architectural treasures was hewn out of the solid rock of the hillside to form a free-standing temple consisting of a gateway, two-storied halls and the main shrine within. The most majestic creation is the Kailash Temple, a full-sized freestanding temple flanked by huge elephants, all carved from solid rock, pillars and podiums, as the workers dug away some 200,000 tons of rock. The result is an awe-inspiring representation of Shiva's Himalayan abode. Nearby caves are alive with stone murals depicting divine struggles and victories. With these caves before us, it is clear that India far surpasses the rest of the world in the glory of its rock-cut architecture.

Main Attraction

Every December, the Ellora festival of music and dance is organized at the Kailasha Temple, which is attended by a large number of people.

CHAPTER 23
Jakhu Temple, Himachal Pradesh

No visit to the state capital Shimla is complete without visiting Jakhu Hill. This hill looms over Shimla town and is the geographical nucleus. This temple is dedicated to the monkey God Hanumana. Jakhu Temple is at east of the town centre near the highest point of the Shimla ridge at 2455 m. A steep 45-minute walk from Scandal Point, it offers fine views over the surrounding valleys out to the snow-capped peaks and over Shimla itself. Jakhu is also a beautiful spot to see the sunrise and sun set. Appropriately, there are many monkeys around the temple.

Legend

No temple in India goes without a legend, Jakhu too has a story. It is said that Hanumana, the faithful ally of Lord Rama of the Ramayana- an epic, was the monkey God with whose help Lord Rama was able to defeat the arch-demon Ravana, the king of Lanka. The faithful nature of Hanumana is often illustrated by his representations being found guarding forts and palace entrances. The British never placed Hanumana on top of Jakhu hill to guard the township. The temple site predates the British Raj.

An episode in the Ramayana had Lakshmana, Rama's brother mortally wounded in a battle with Ravana's forces. Hanumana was sent to fetch the mythical medicinal herb called 'Sanjivini' from the Himalayas in order to cure the wounded Lakshmana. The legend about the temple is that Hanumana rested at Jakhu

Hill after collecting the herb. After resting, he journeyed back to the battlefield of Lanka. There are many monkeys around the temple, but surprisingly they don't attack people unless fiddled with. Pilgrims offer them eatables, which they readily accept.

The approach to the temple is through a dense forest of Deodars. Though many find the climb tiresome, ponies are available for a to and fro ride to the temple. The path towards the temple starts just left of Christ Church. After the hard hack up, the temple itself, a red and yellow brick affair crammed with fairy lights and tinsel, comes as something of an anti climax. The shrine inside houses are believed to be the footprints of Hanumana.

But the monkeys can be a bit troublesome, so be careful and keep food out of sight and reach. For those who need a helping hand with the climb, walking sticks are available at teashops at the base.

CHAPTER 24
Jagannath Temple, Orissa

Lord of The Universe

In the minds of the millions of Indians, Orissa is the land of Jagannath. The name Jagannath literally means 'Lord of the Universe'. It is one of the most sacred pilgrimage spots in India and it is also one of the four abodes (dhamas) of the divine that lie on the four directions of the compass. The Jagannath temple in Puri was built approximately in 1135-1150 by King Chodaganga of the Eastern Ganga dynasty and finished by his descendant, Anangabhima Deva, during the 12th century. This was during the classical period of temple building in Orissa (approximately the eighth through thirteenth centuries). One of the most revered of all temples of Lord Vishnu is the Lord Jagannath Temple in eastern India.

The temple is dedicated to Jagannath, who is identified by his devotees with Krishna. It is also dedicated to Balabhadra and Subhadra, the brother and sister, respectively, of Jagannath. These three together are the principal deities of the temple, whose images reside in the temple's sanctuary. Like the Lingaraja temple in Bhubaneshwar, this temple too is not open for Non-Hindus who contend themselves by viewing it from outside its precincts.

Main Attraction

A famous festival related to the Jagannath temple is the ratha yatra or chariot festival, which occurs yearly in June or July. During the Rath Yatra Festival, the images of Jagannatha,

Balabhadra and Subhadra are placed in mammoth chariots or 'raths', the largest of which is 14 meters (46 feet) high and has 16 wheels, each more than two meters (seven feet) in diameter, which are then drawn along Grand Road to the Gundecha temple, a few kilometers away. After they have stayed in that temple for seven days, the deities again ride the chariots back to their home temple. This journey commemorates that of Lord Krishna from Gokul to Mathura.

Mahaprasada

Mahaprasada is pure vegetarian spiritual food offered to Lord Jagannath. Just by eating this mahaprasada one makes great spiritual advancement. Everyday, fifty-six varieties of prasada are offered to Lord Jagannath. The preparations are made traditionally and no onion, garlic, chillies and many other varieties of vegetables (considered alien) are not used. These offerings are first made to Lord Jagannath then they are in turn offered to Goddess Bimala Devi in the temple precincts and then becomes Mahaprasadam. This Mahaprasadam is considered very efficacious for spiritual liberation. One should respectfully honour the Mahaprasadam sitting on the floor. This Mahaprasadam is available daily between 3 -5 pm. This is sold outside the sanctorum area but within the temple premises. The Mahaprasadam remains hot for a long time as it is kept in the same earthen pots, which are used to cook it.

Most probably it may be rice, make it clear how much you want while ordering. Even if you say it ten times, you will probably be brought way too much the first time. Normally, maha-prasada means a few small pots of sabji (vegetables), dhal and a pot of rice ten times the size of the small sabji pots.